Phillips, Craig & Dean — top of my lungs

ISBN 13: 978-1-4234-2360-7
ISBN 10: 1-4234-2360-7

7777 W. BLUEMOUND RD. P.O. BOX 13819 MILWAUKEE, WI 53213

For all works contained herein:
Unauthorized copying, arranging, adapting, recording or public performance is an infringement of copyright.
Infringers are liable under the law.

Visit Hal Leonard Online at
www.halleonard.com

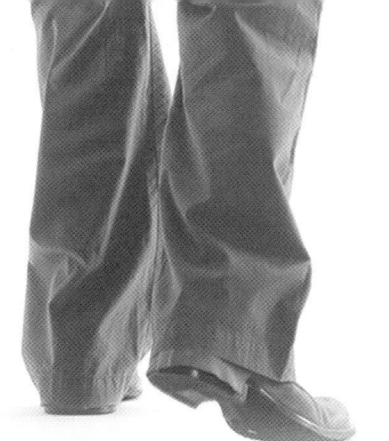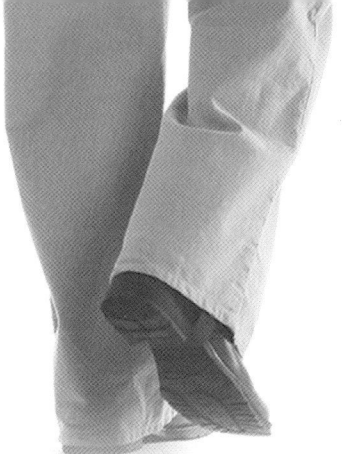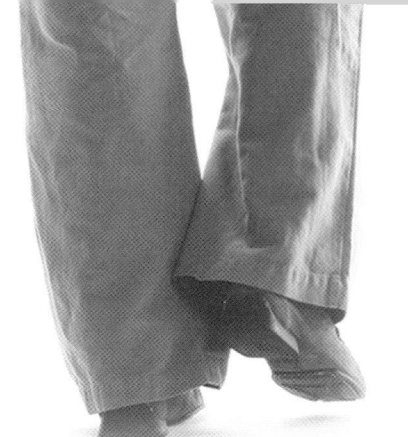

CONTENTS

- 4 ONE WAY
- 11 YOUR NAME
- 18 TOP OF MY LUNGS
- 24 SAVED THE DAY
- 30 AMAZED
- 35 I WILL BOAST
- 44 BECAUSE OF THAT BLOOD
- 52 LET THE REDEEMED
- 60 THAT'S MY LORD
- 66 FOR YOUR GLORY

ONE WAY

Words and Music by JOEL HOUSTON
and JONATHAN DOUGLASS

*Recorded a half step lower.

© 2003 Joel Houston, Jonathan Douglass and Hillsong Publishing (admin. in the United States and Canada by Integrity's Hosanna! Music/ASCAP)
c/o Integrity Media, Inc., 1000 Cody Road, Mobile, AL 36695
All Rights Reserved   International Copyright Secured   Used by Permission

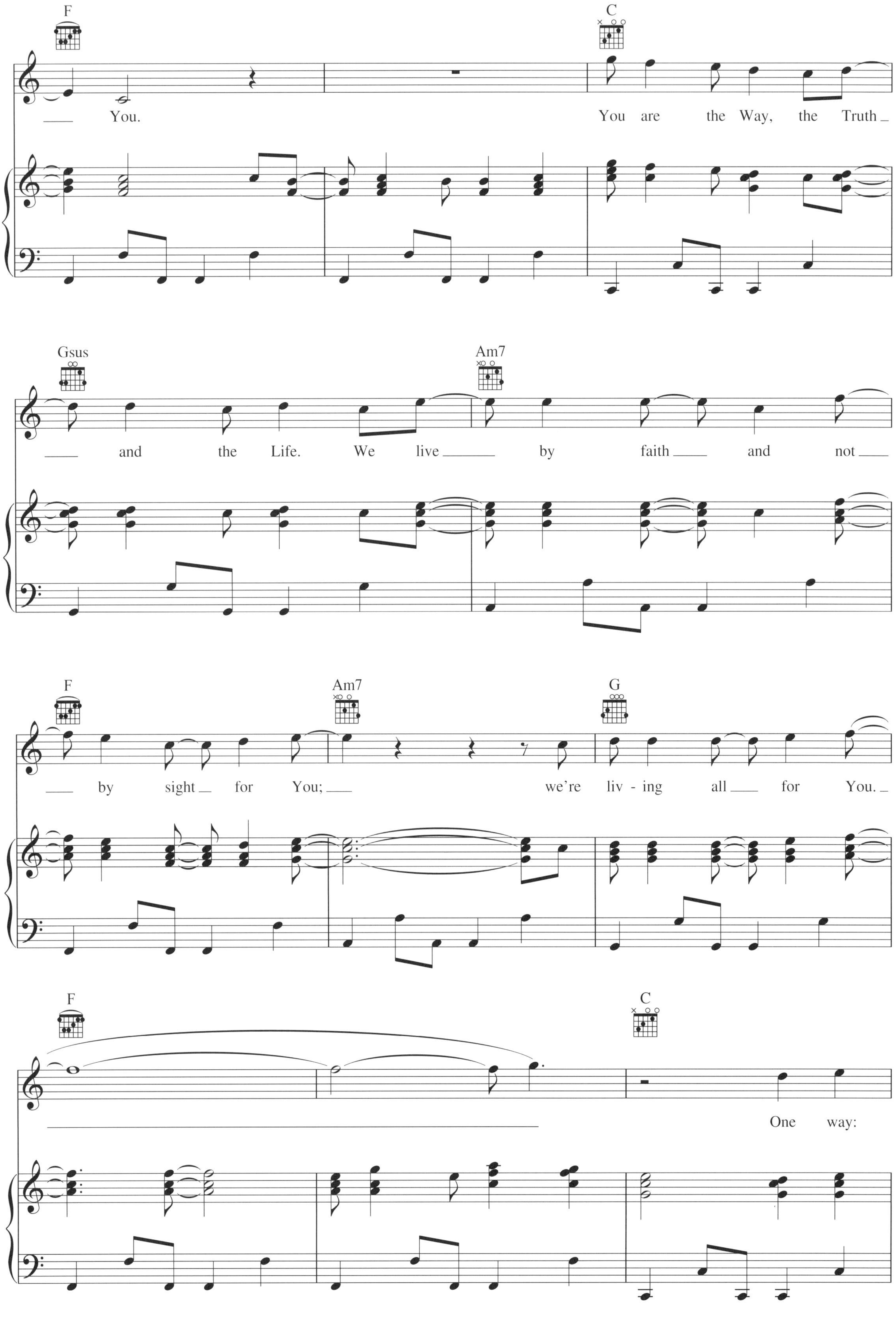
F
C
You. You are the Way, the Truth
Gsus
Am7
and the Life. We live by faith and not
F
Am7
G
by sight for You; we're liv - ing all for You.
F
C
One way:

YOUR NAME

Words and Music by PAUL BALOCHE and GLEN PACKLAM

*Recorded a half step lower.

© 2006 Integrity's Hosanna! Music/ASCAP and Vertical Worship Songs/ASCAP
c/o Integrity Media, Inc., 1000 Cody Road, Mobile, AL 36695
All Rights Reserved   International Copyright Secured   Used by Permission

TOP OF MY LUNGS

Words and Music by TONY WOOD,
RYAN WINGO and JIM ODOM

SAVED THE DAY

Words and Music by
MICHAEL NEALE

© 2005 Integrity's Praise! Music/BMI
c/o Integrity Media, Inc., 1000 Cody Road, Mobile, AL 36695
All Rights Reserved   International Copyright Secured   Used by Permission

I WILL BOAST

Words and Music by
PAUL BALOCHE

© 2006 Integrity's Hosanna! Music/ASCAP
c/o Integrity Media, Inc., 1000 Cody Road, Mobile, AL 36695
All Rights Reserved   International Copyright Secured   Used by Permission

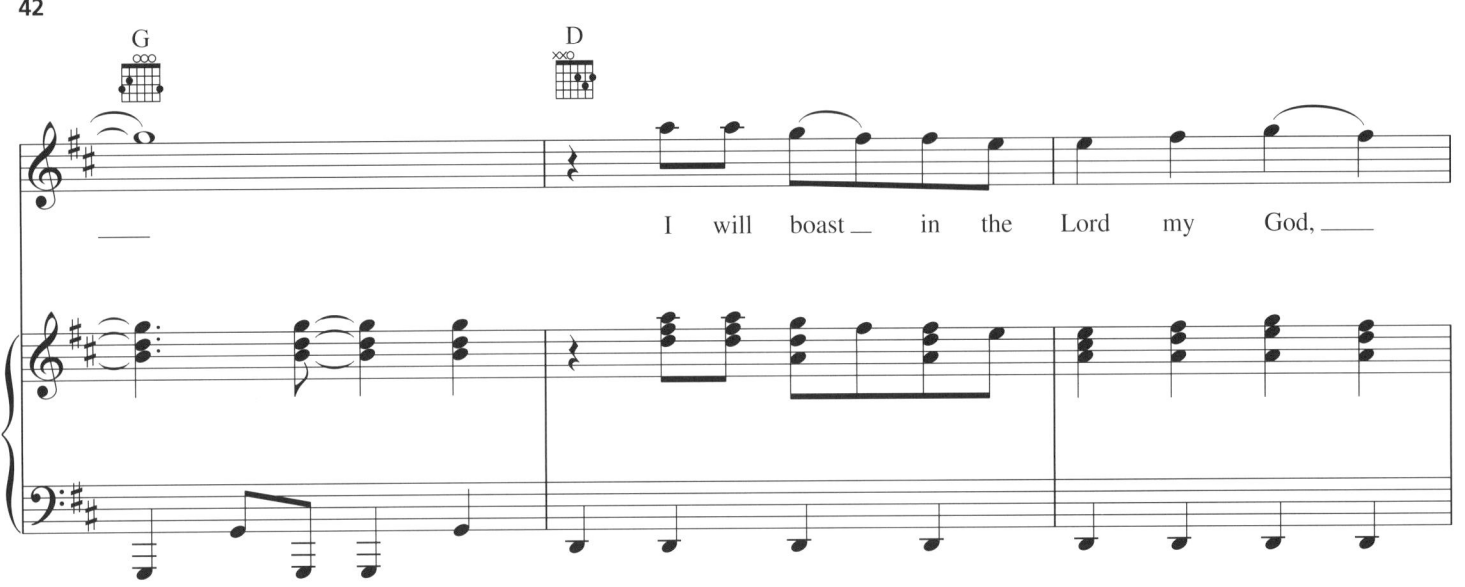

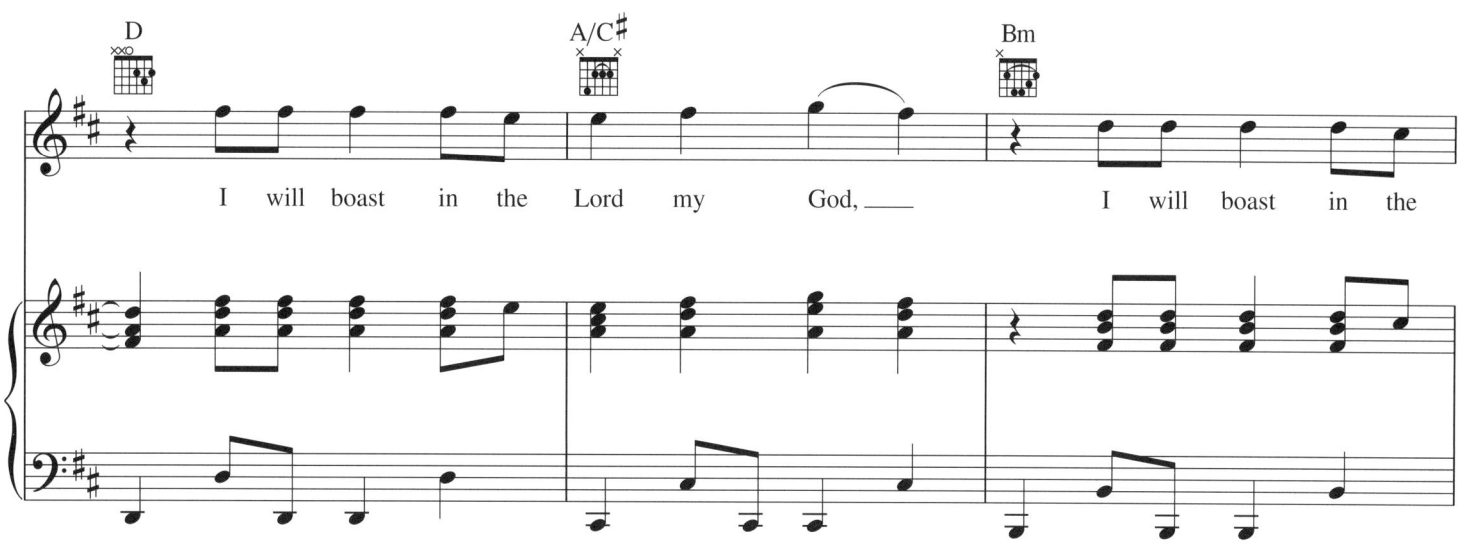
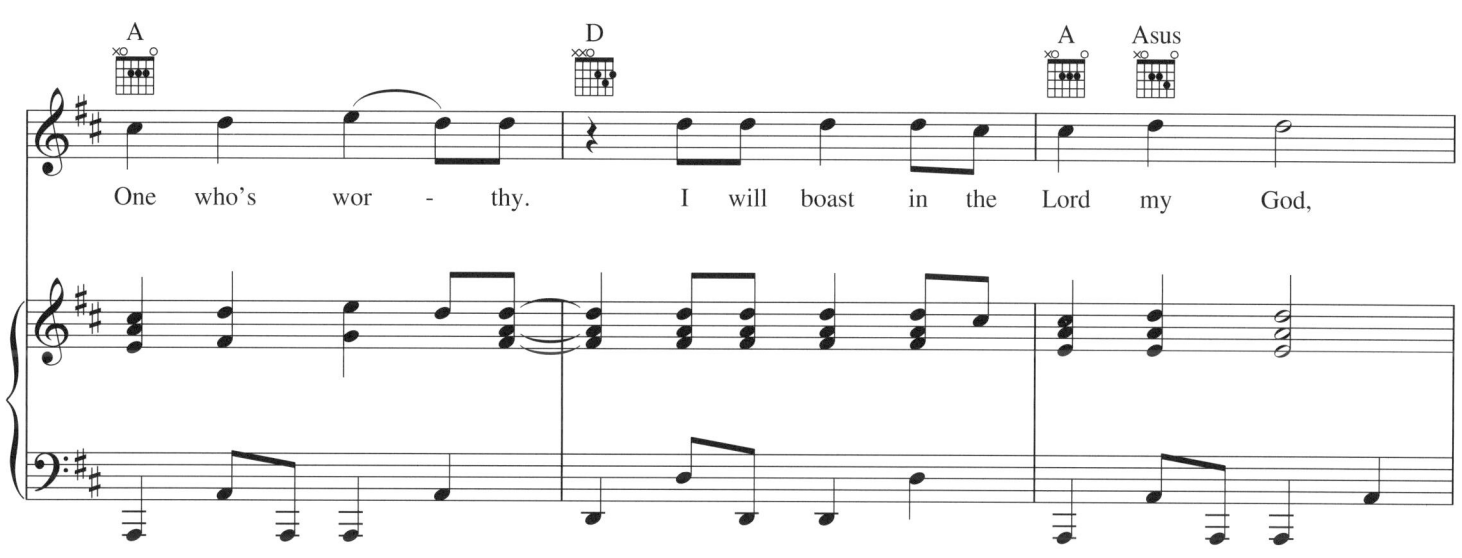

BECAUSE OF THAT BLOOD

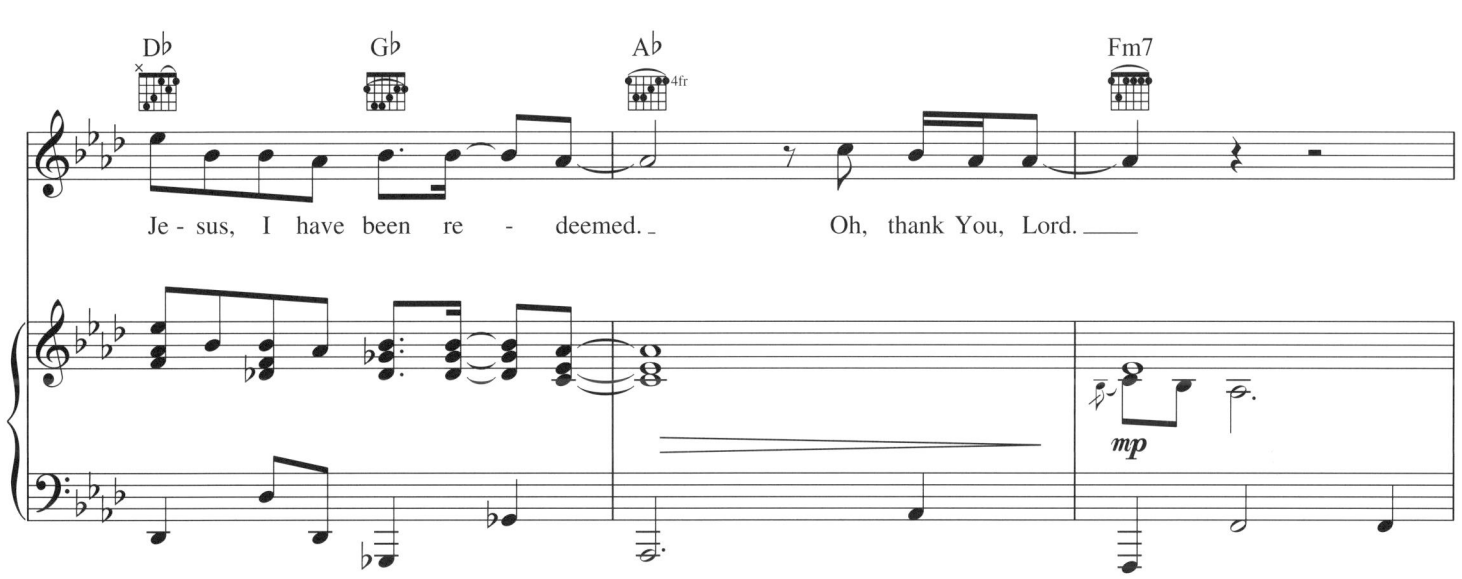

LET THE REDEEMED

Words and Music by DAN DEAN
and ROGER HODGES

Moderate Rock beat

Freedom's song is loud-
Arms of love feel strong-

-est if you've lived a life of chains.
-est when you've been so all a- lone.

© 2006 Dudedabe Music/ASCAP (admin. by Integrity's Hosanna! Music), Integrity's Hosanna! Music/ASCAP
(both c/o Integrity Media, Inc., 1000 Cody Road, Mobile, AL 36695) and Big God Music/BMI
All Rights Reserved   International Copyright Secured   Used by Permission

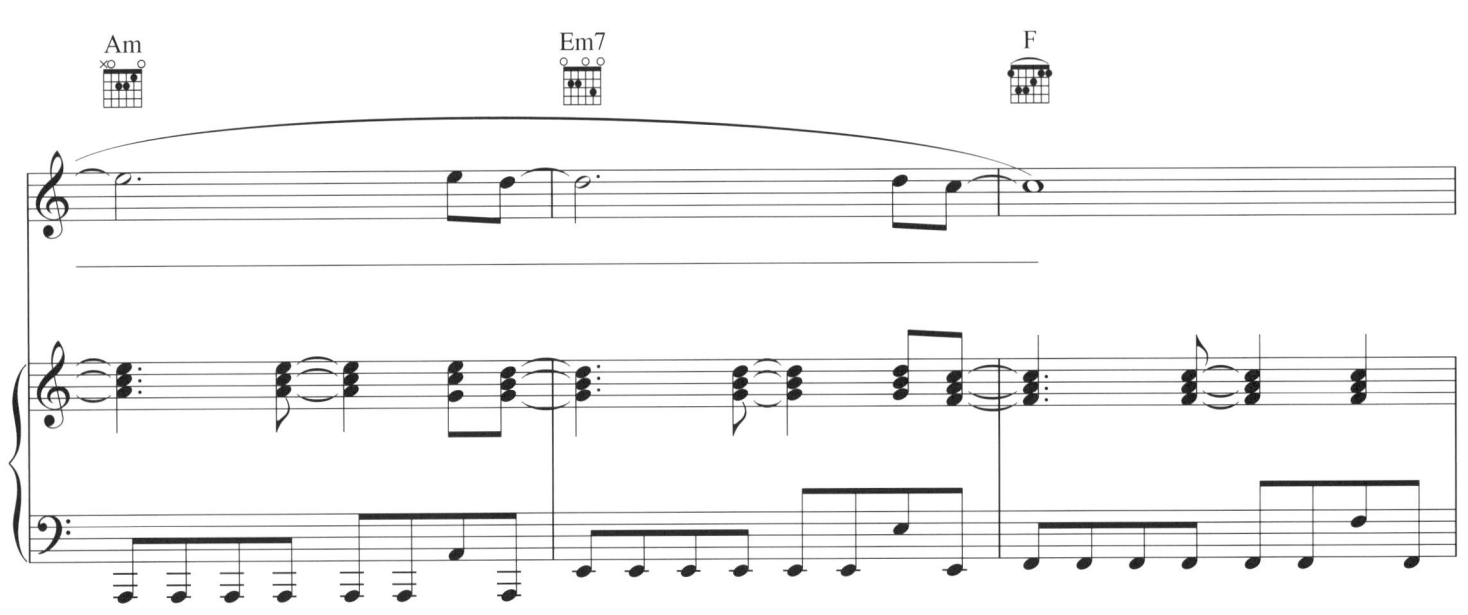
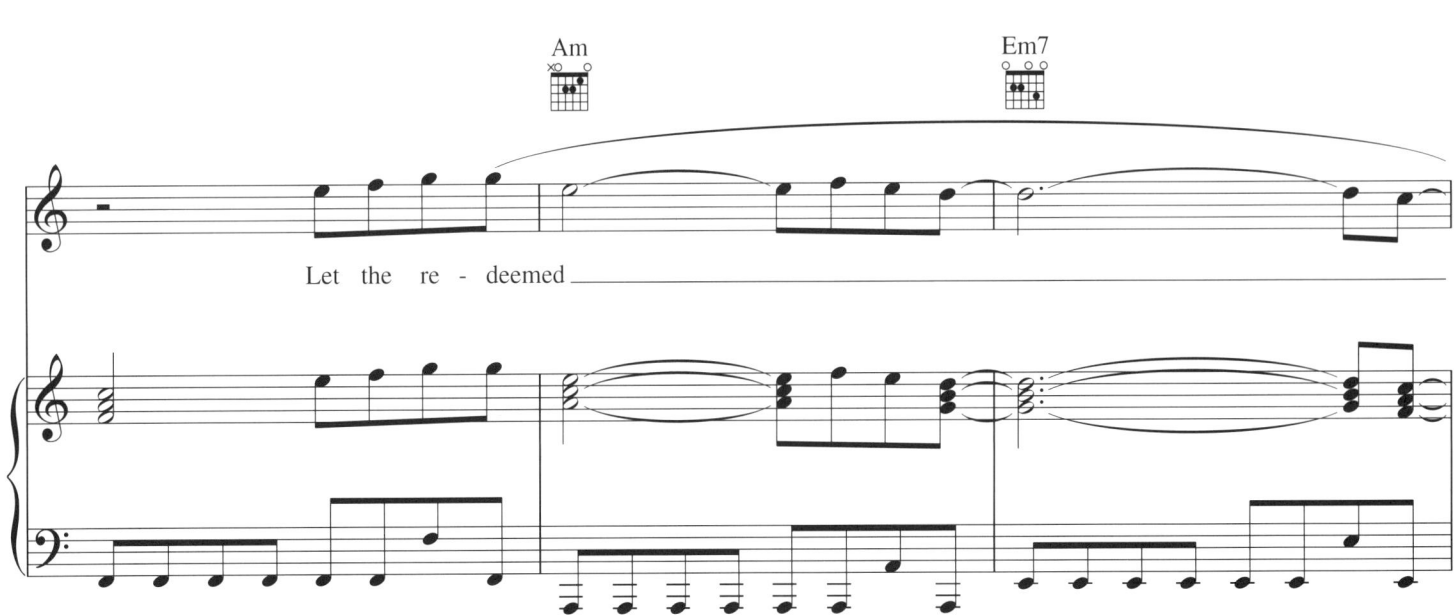

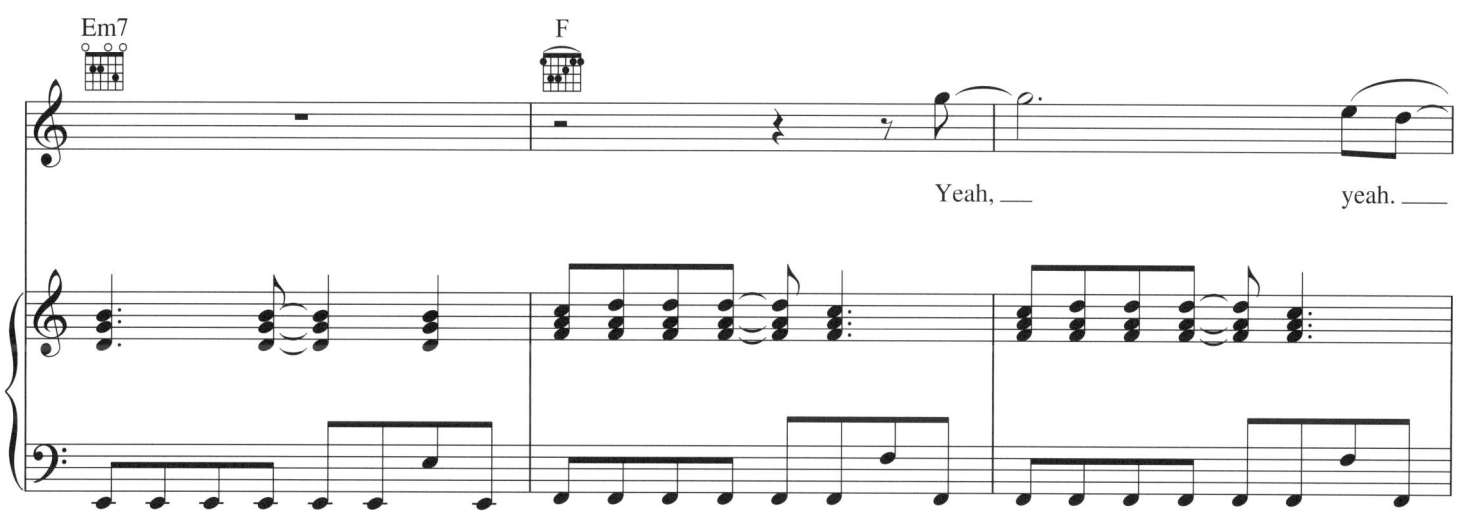
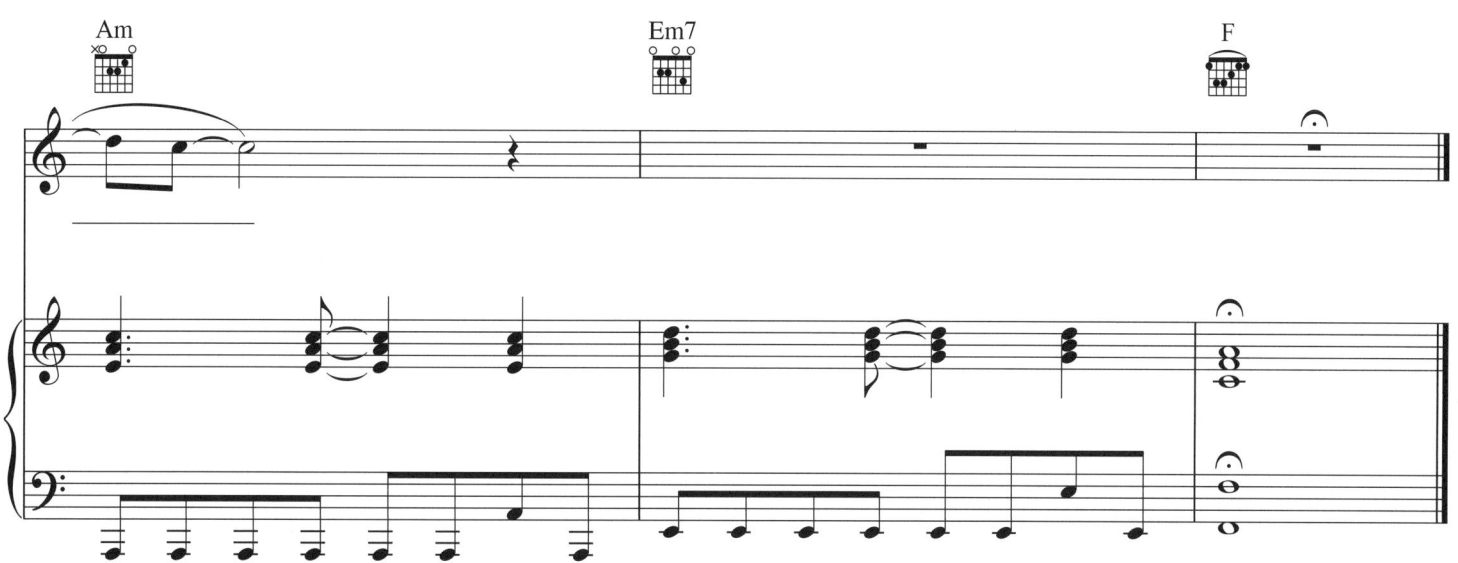

THAT'S MY LORD

Words and Music by SHAWN CRAIG
and ROGER HODGES

© 2006 PraiseSong Press/ASCAP (admin. by Integrity's Hosanna! Music), Integrity's Hosanna! Music/ASCAP
(both c/o Integrity Media, Inc., 1000 Cody Road, Mobile, AL 36695) and Big God Music/BMI
All Rights Reserved   International Copyright Secured   Used by Permission

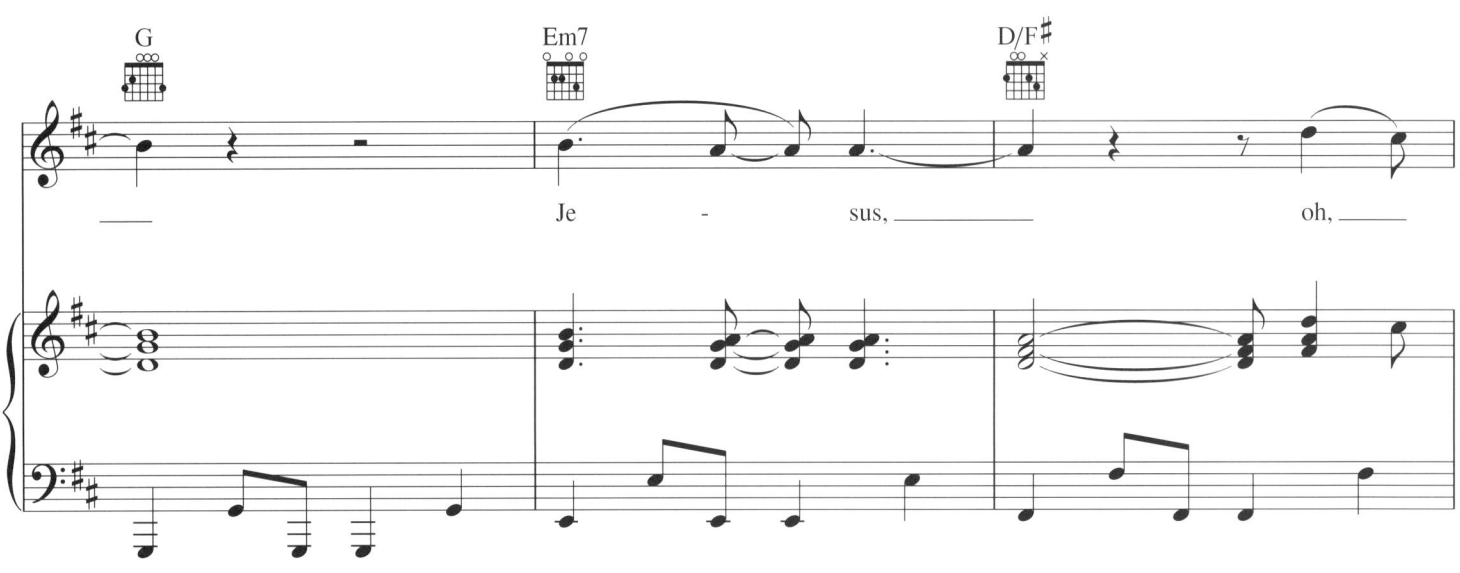
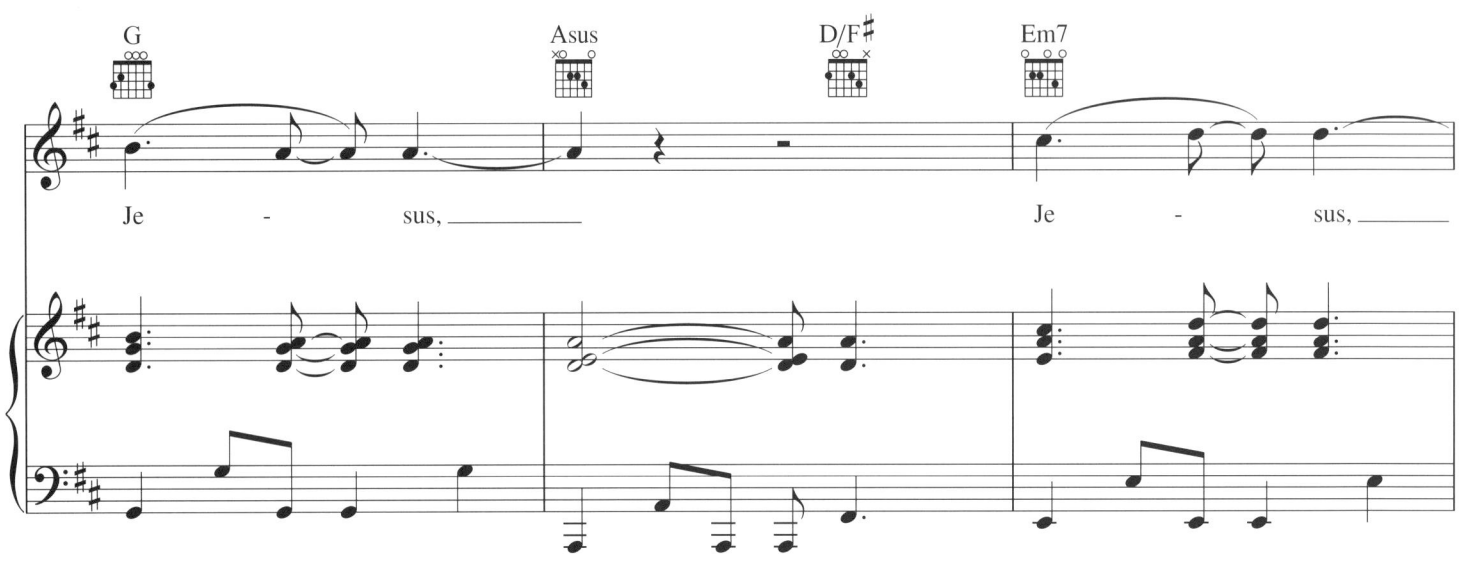
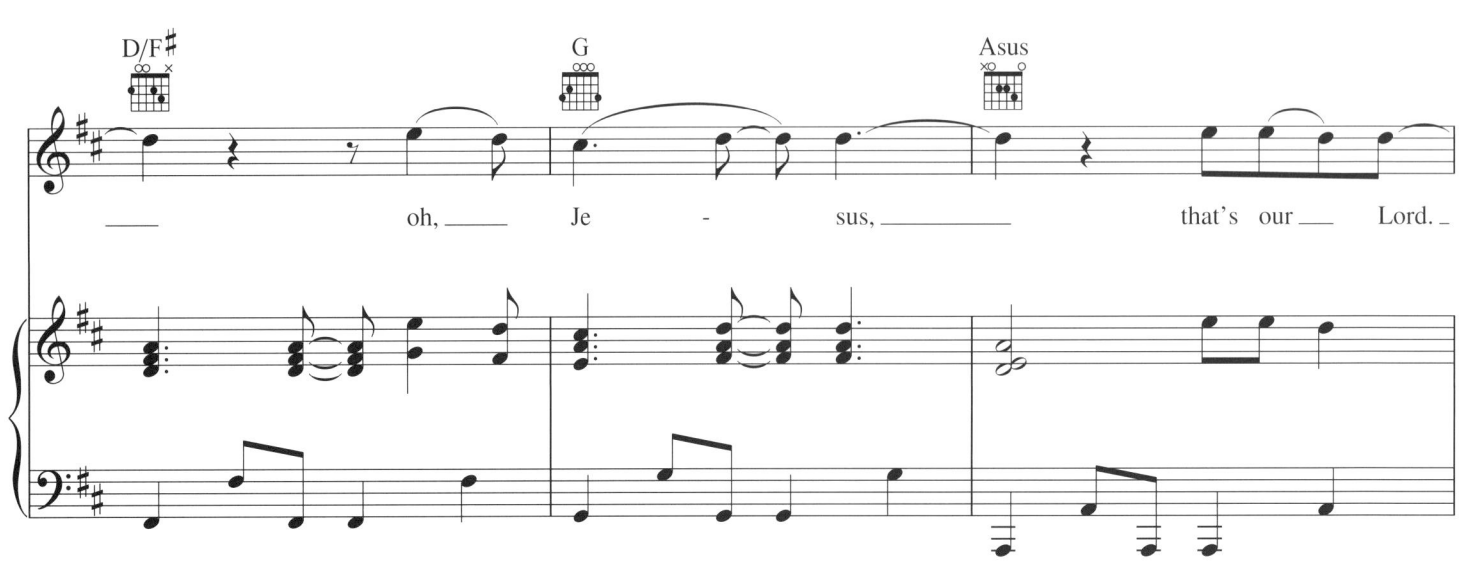

FOR YOUR GLORY

Words and Music by
MATT MAHER

© 2006 THANKYOU MUSIC (PRS) and SPIRITANDSONG.COM PUBLISHING (BMI)
THANKYOU MUSIC Admin. Worldwide by EMI CMG PUBLISHING excluding Europe which is Admin. by kingswaysongs.com
SPIRITANDSONG.COM PUBLISHING Admin. by EMI CMG PUBLISHING
All Rights Reserved   Used by Permission

THE BEST PRAISE & WORSHIP SONGBOOKS

THE BEST OF PAUL BALOCHE – OPEN THE EYES OF MY HEART
This songbook features 12 of Paul's best praise & worship favorites: Above All • All the Earth Will Sing Your Praises • Arise • Celebrate the Lord of Love • I Love to Be in Your Presence • I See the Lord • Offering • Open the Eyes of My Heart • Praise Adonai • Revival Fire Fall • Rise Up and Praise Him • Sing Out.
08739746 Piano/Vocal/Guitar $14.95

THE BEST OF HILLSONG
25 of the most popular songs from Hillsong artists and writers, including: All Things Are Possible • Awesome in This Place • Blessed • Eagle's Wings • God Is Great • Holy Spirit Rain Down • I Give You My Heart • Jesus, What a Beautiful Name • The Potter's Hand • Shout to the Lord • Worthy Is the Lamb • You Are Near • and more.
08739789 Piano/Vocal/Guitar $16.95

THE BEST OF INTEGRITY MUSIC
25 of the best praise & worship songs from Integrity: Ancient of Days • Celebrate Jesus • Firm Foundation • Give Thanks • Mighty Is Our God • Open the Eyes of My Heart • Trading My Sorrows • You Are Good • and more.
08739790 Piano/Vocal/Guitar $16.95

THE BEST OF MODERN WORSHIP
15 of today's most powerful worship songs: Cannot Say Enough • Everyday • Fields of Grace • Freedom • Friend of God • God Is Great • Here I Am to Worship • I Can Only Imagine • Lord, You Have My Heart • Meet with Me • Open the Eyes of My Heart • Sing for Joy • Trading My Sorrows • Word of God Speak • You Are My King (Amazing Love).
08739747 Piano/Vocal/Guitar $14.95

COME INTO HIS PRESENCE
Features 12 beautiful piano solo arrangements of worship favorites: Above All • Blessed Be the Lord God Almighty • Breathe • Come Into His Presence • Draw Me Close • Give Thanks • God Will Make a Way • Jesus, Name Above All Names/Blessed Be the Name of the Lord • Lord Have Mercy • More Precious Than Silver • Open the Eyes of My Heart • Shout to the Lord.
08739299 Piano Solo $12.95

GIVE THANKS – THE BEST OF HOSANNA! MUSIC
This superb best-of collection features 25 worship favorites published by Hosanna! Music: Ancient of Days • Celebrate Jesus • I Worship You, Almighty God • More Precious Than Silver • My Redeemer Lives • Shout to the Lord • and more.
08739729 Piano/Vocal/Guitar $14.95
08739745 Easy Piano $12.95

iWORSHIP CHRISTMAS
Selections from the popular Christmas album, including: Away in a Manger • The Birthday of a King • Breath of Heaven (Mary's Song) • Come, Thou Long-Expected Jesus • Hallelujah • Joy to the World/Heaven and Nature Sing • One Small Child/More Precious Than Silver • What Child Is This? • You Are Emmanuel/Emmanuel • and more.
08739788 Piano/Vocal/Guitar $16.95

THE SONGS OF MERCYME – I CAN ONLY IMAGINE
10 of the most recognizable songs from this popular Contemporary Christian group, including the smash hit "I Can Only Imagine," plus: Cannot Say Enough • Here with Me • Homesick • How Great Is Your Love • The Love of God • Spoken For • Unaware • Where You Lead Me • Word of God Speak.
08739803 Piano Solo $12.95

MERCYME – 20 FAVORITES
A jam-packed collection of 20 of their best. Includes: Crazy • Go • Here with Me • I Can Only Imagine • In the Blink of an Eye • Never Alone • On My Way to You • Spoken For • Undone • Word of God Speak • Your Glory Goes On • and more.
08739862 Piano/Vocal/Guitar $17.95

Prices, contents & availability subject to change without notice.

FOR MORE INFORMATION, SEE YOUR LOCAL MUSIC DEALER, OR WRITE TO:

7777 W. BLUEMOUND RD. P.O. BOX 13819 MILWAUKEE, WI 53213

Complete songlists available online at
www.halleonard.com

MIGHTY IS OUR GOD
25 beloved praise & worship songs, including: Above All • Firm Foundation • I Stand in Awe • Lord Most High • Open the Eyes of My Heart • Sing for Joy • Think About His Love • and more.
08739744 Piano/Vocal/Guitar $14.95

THE BEST OF DON MOEN – GOD WILL MAKE A WAY
19 of the greatest hits from this Dove Award-winning singer/songwriter. Includes: Celebrate Jesus • God Will Make a Way • Here We Are • I Will Sing • Let Your Glory Fall • Shout to the Lord • We Give You Glory • You Make Me Lie Down in Green Pastures • and more.
08739297 Piano/Vocal/Guitar $16.95

PHILLIPS, CRAIG & DEAN – LET THE WORSHIPPERS ARISE
12 songs from the 2004 release by this trio of pastors. Includes: Because I'm Forgiven • You Are God Alone • Let the Worshippers Arise • My Redeemer Lives • Awake My Soul • Mighty Is the Power of the Cross • and more.
08739804 Piano/Vocal/Guitar $16.95

PIANO PRAISE
This flexible book features 8 songs for performing in church as a soloist or at home for personal worship. Includes optional instrumental obbligato parts, chord symbols for improvisation, and a CD with play-along tracks and demonstrations. Includes: Firm Foundation • Jesus, Name Above All Names • More Precious Than Silver • Open the Eyes of My Heart • and more.
08739851 Piano Solo – Book/CD Pack $19.95

VOICES OF PRAISE
10 worship favorites arranged especially for vocalists, including: God Will Make a Way • Here I Am to Worship • Open the Eyes of My Heart • and more. The CD includes vocal demonstrations as well as accompaniment tracks.
08739801 Medium Voice – Book/CD Pack $19.95

DARLENE ZSCHECH – WORTHY IS THE LAMB
15 songs from this contemporary worship leader, including: Blessed • Hallelujah • Irresistible • Kiss of Heaven • Let the Peace of God Reign • The Potter's Hand • Shout to the Lord • Worthy Is the Lamb • and more.
08739852 Piano/Vocal/Guitar $16.95